Rose is Rose
Right on the Lips

Pat Brady

**Andrews McMeel
Publishing**

Kansas City

Rose is Rose is distributed internationally by United Feature Syndicate, Inc.

Rose is Rose Right on the Lips copyright © 2003 by United Feature Syndicate, Inc. All rights reserved. Printed in the United States of America. No part of this book may be used or reproduced in any manner whatsoever without written permission except in the case of reprints in the context of reviews. For information, write Andrews McMeel Publishing, an Andrews McMeel Universal company, 4520 Main Street, Kansas City, Missouri 64111.

03 04 05 06 07 BBG 10 9 8 7 6 5 4 3 2 1

ISBN: 0-7407-3955-7

Library of Congress Control Number: 2003106497

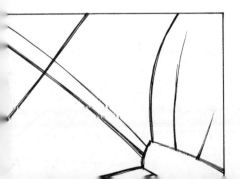

More *Rose is Rose* collections are available everywhere, including on the
Rose is Rose Web site at www.roseisrose.com

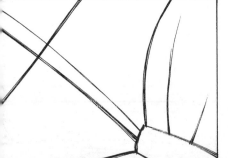

Flip the page corners
and watch both sides!

Flip the page corners
and watch both sides!

7

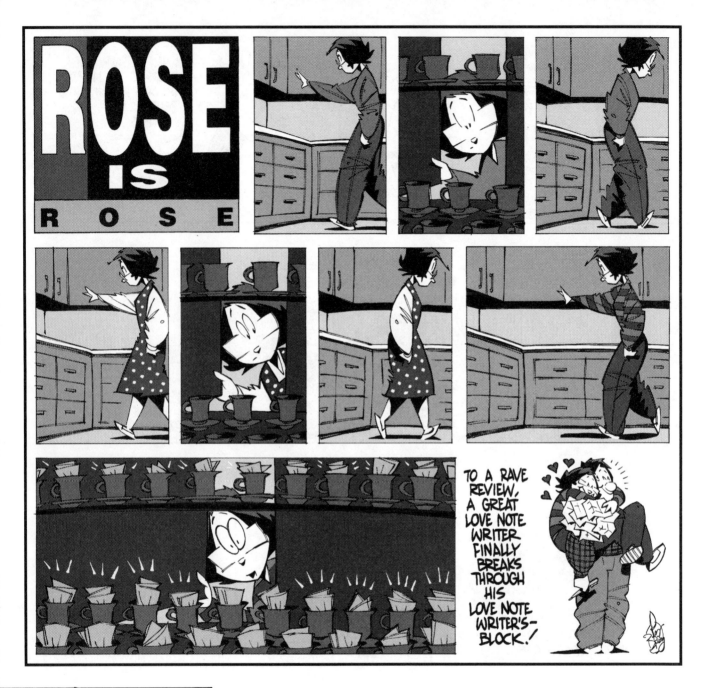

9

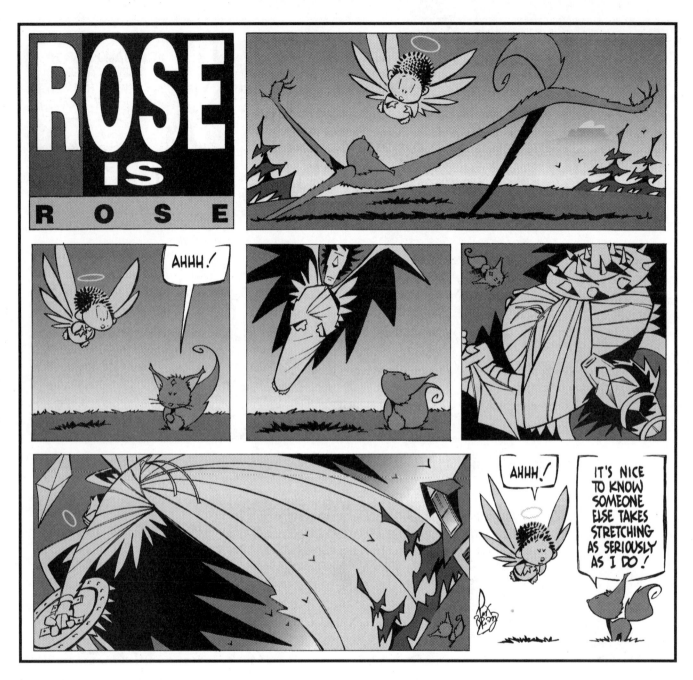

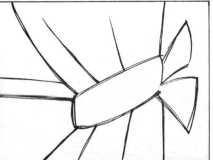

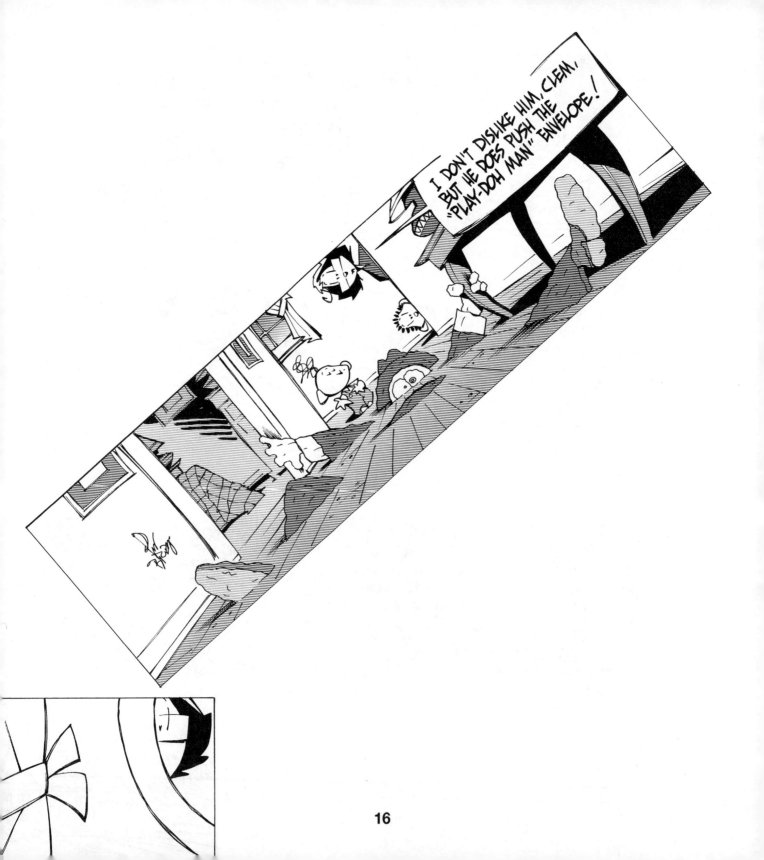

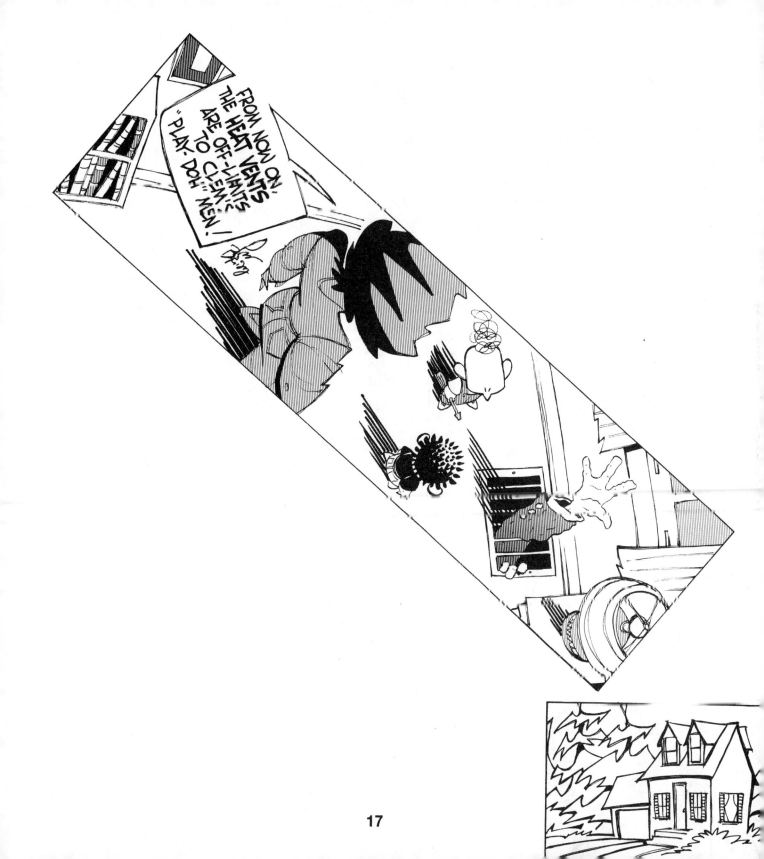

21

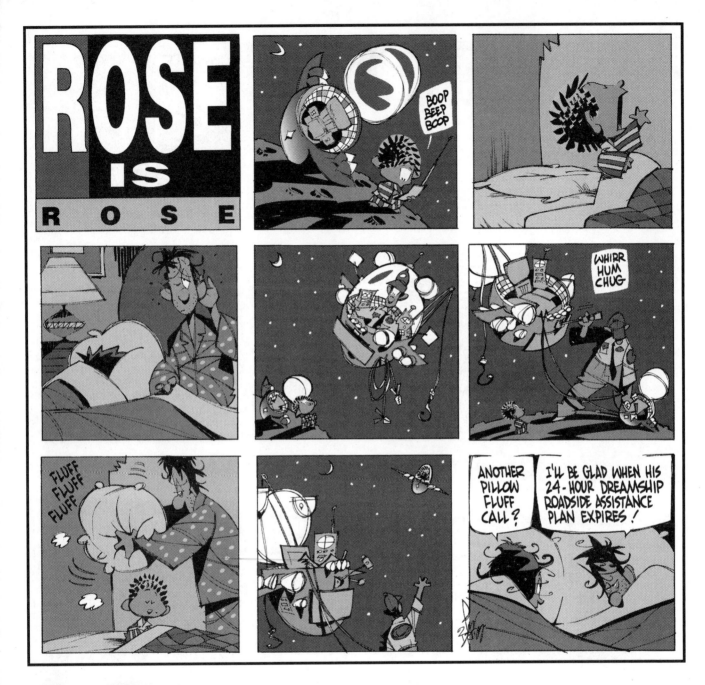

Flip the page corners
and watch both sides!

Flip the page corners
and watch both sides!

29

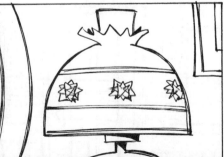

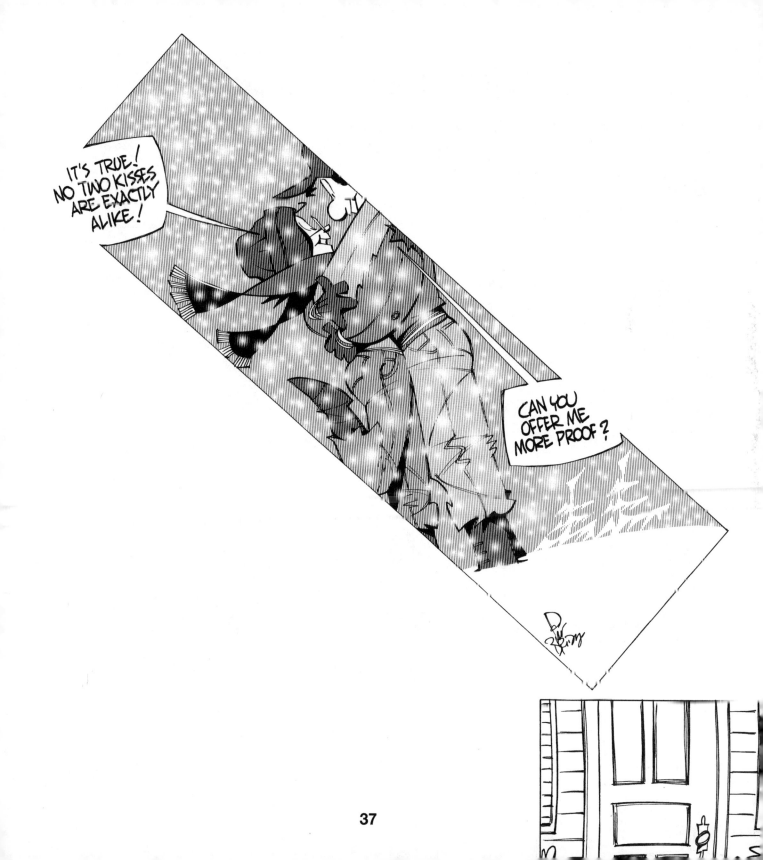

41

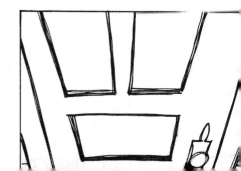

43

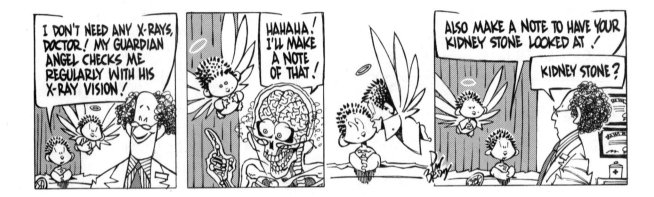

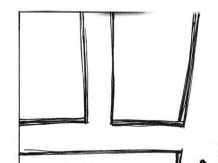

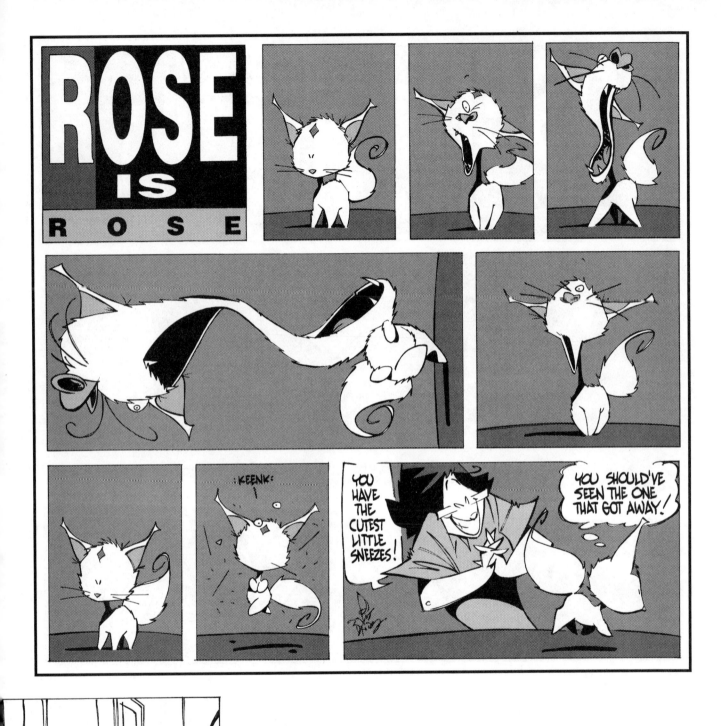

48

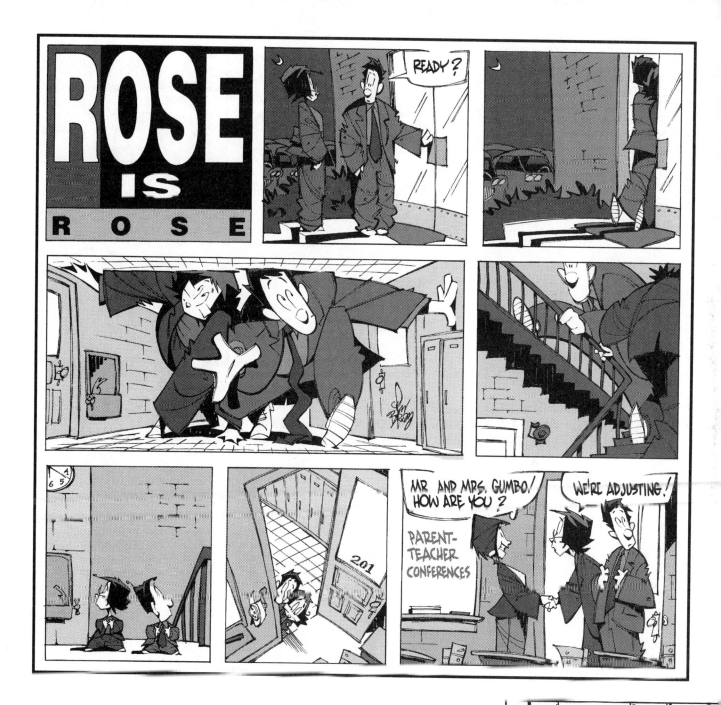

Flip the page corners and watch both sides!

Flip the page corners
and watch both sides!

64

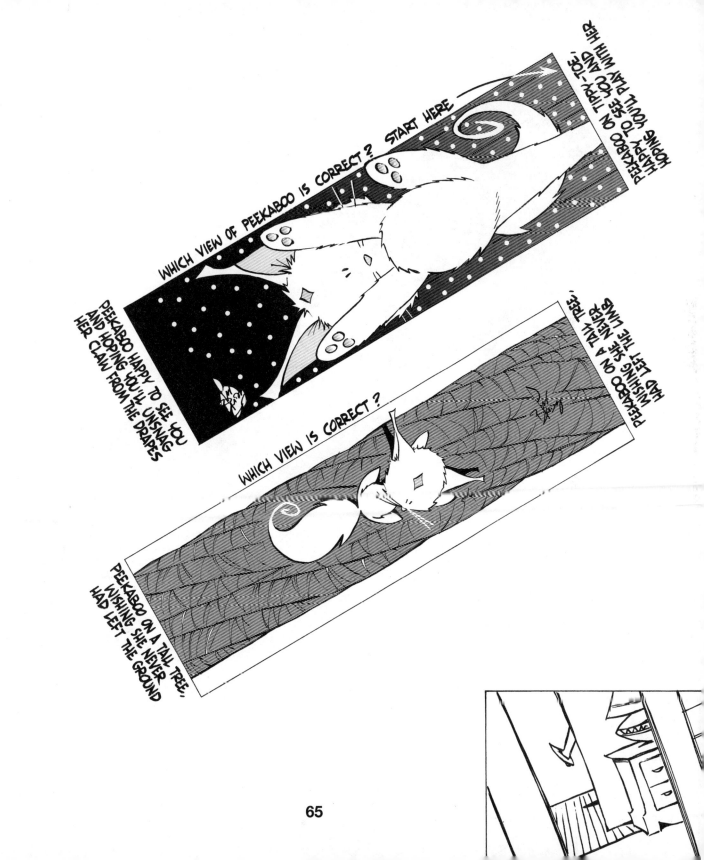

WHICH VIEW OF PEEKABOO IS CORRECT? START HERE

PEEKABOO ON TIPPY-TOE, HAPPY TO SEE YOU AND HOPING YOU'LL PLAY WITH HER

PEEKABOO HAPPY TO SEE YOU AND HOPING YOU'LL UNSNAG HER CLAW FROM THE DRAPES

WHICH VIEW IS CORRECT?

PEEKABOO ON A TALL TREE, WISHING SHE NEVER HAD LEFT THE LIMB

PEEKABOO ON A TALL TREE, WISHING SHE NEVER HAD LEFT THE GROUND

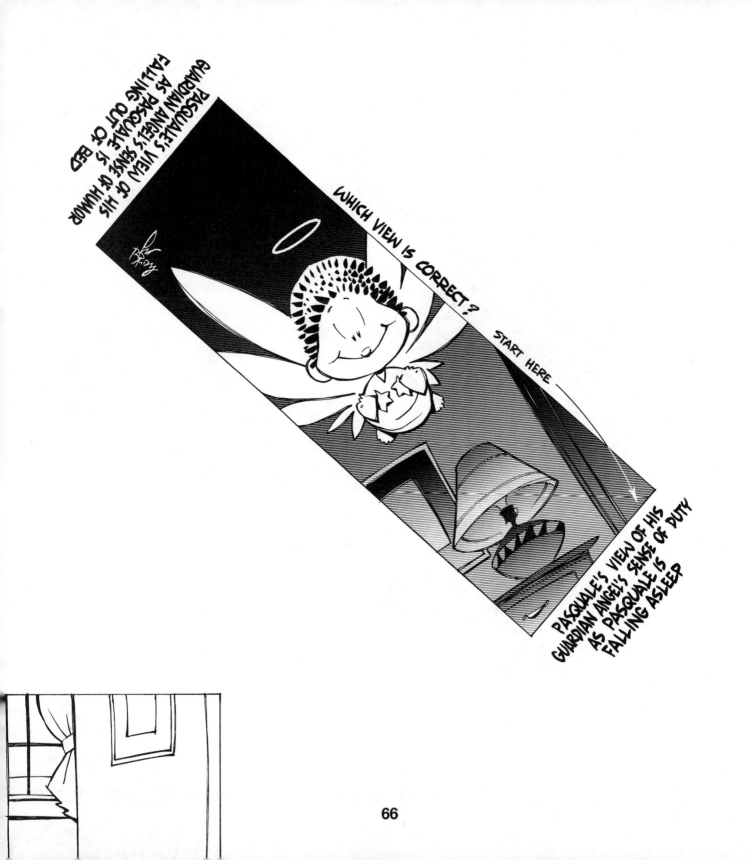

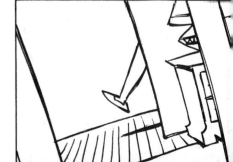

A CLAW SNAG PROBLEM CAN BE COMPOUNDED IF MISINTERPRETED AS A PIGGYBACK RIDE INVITATION.

EVERYBODY KNOWS IF YOU WANT A JOB DONE WELL, YOU GIVE IT TO THE BUSIEST WORKER.

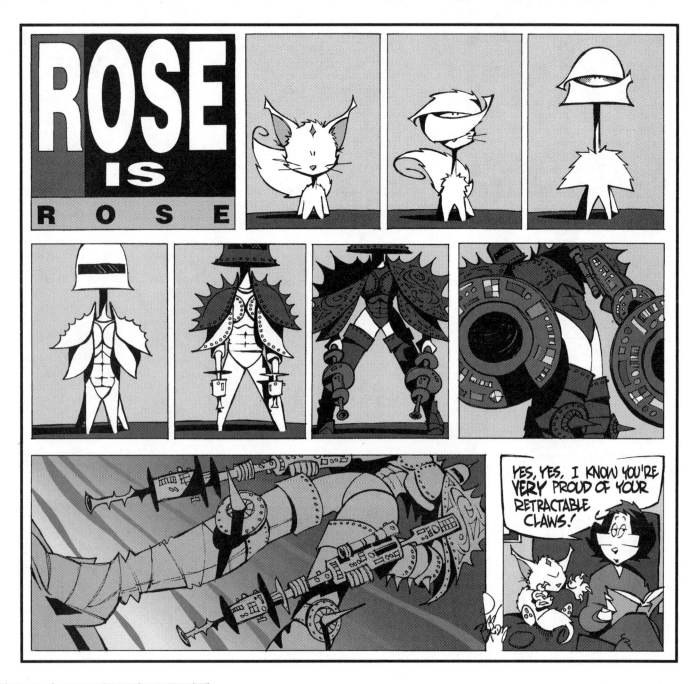

Hate the Snub,
Love the Snubber.

Flip the page corners
and watch both sides!

**Flip the page corners
and watch both sides!**

75

WISDOM FROM MAHARISHI PEEKABOO:

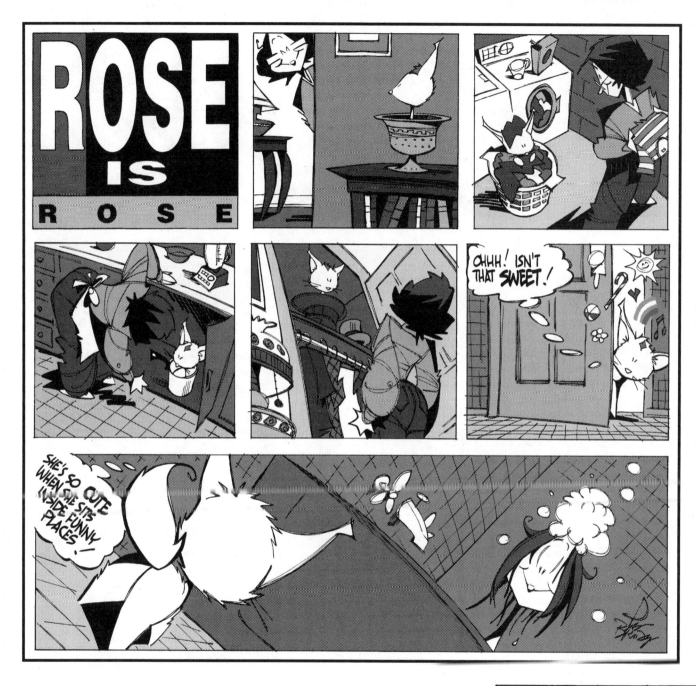

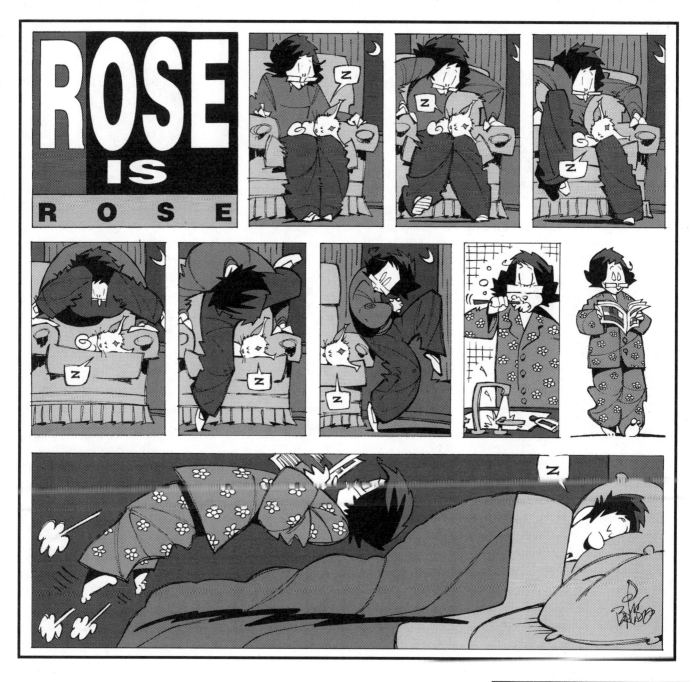

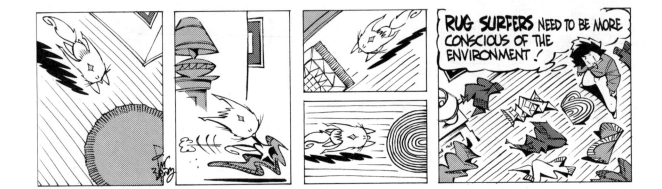

95

TODAY'S FORECAST CALLS FOR MOSTLY SMILEY FACES, WITH SCATTERED FROWN FLURRIES BUT NO ACCUMULATION.

99

Flip the page corners
and watch both sides!

Flip the page corners
and watch both sides!

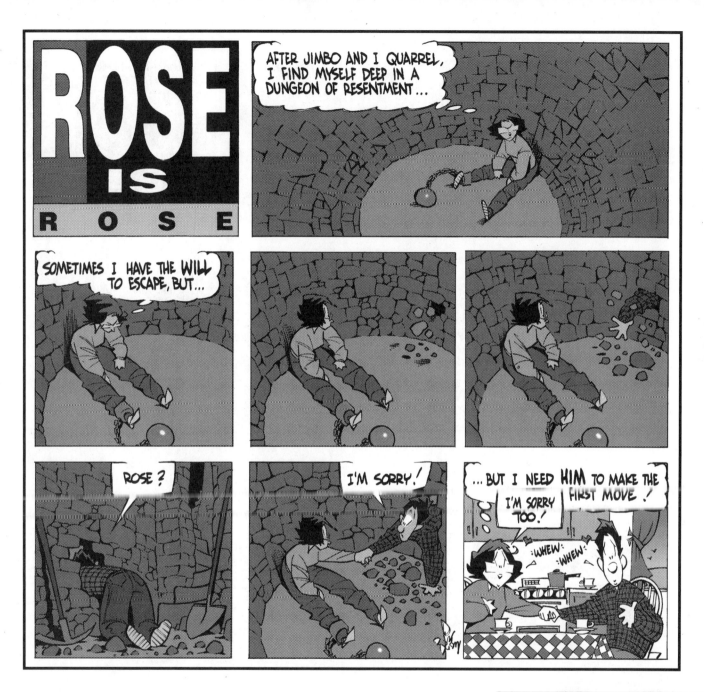

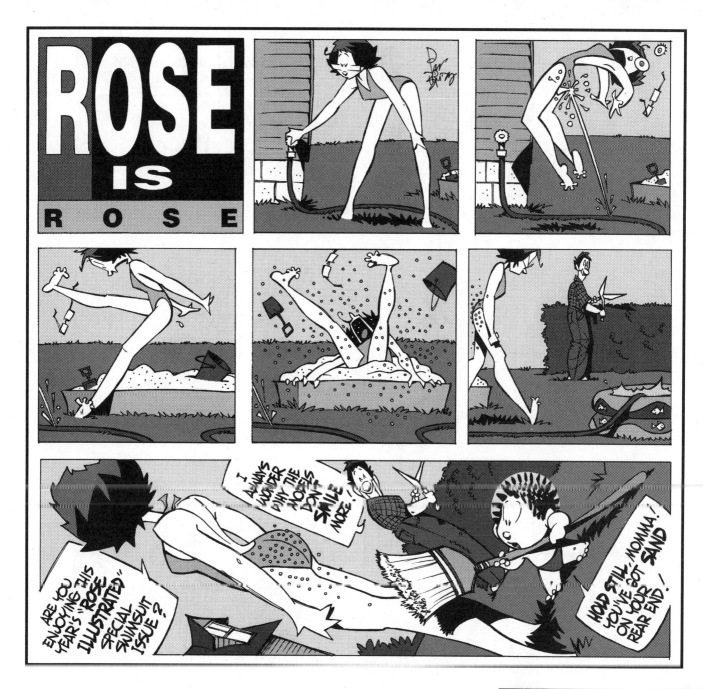

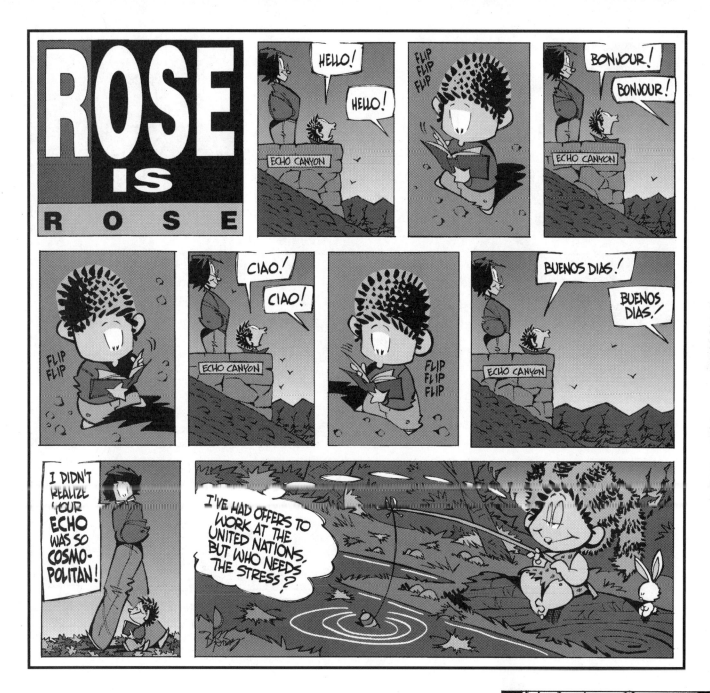

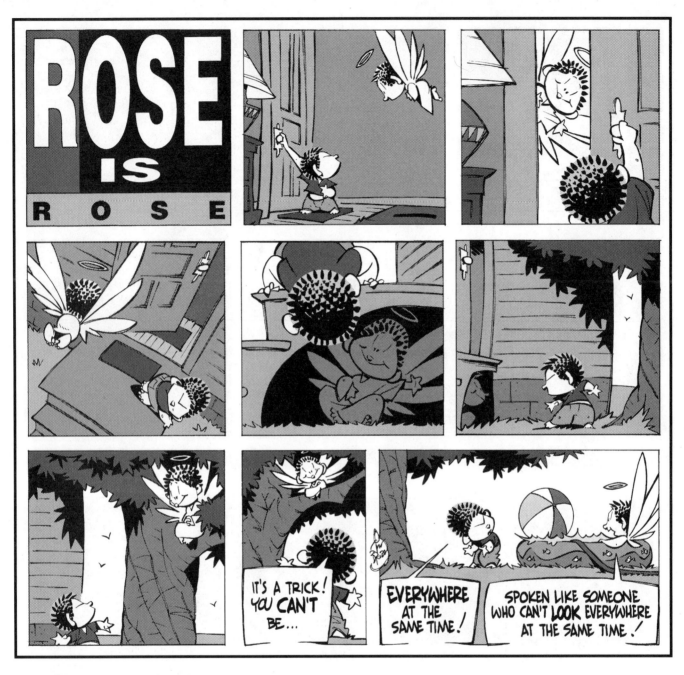

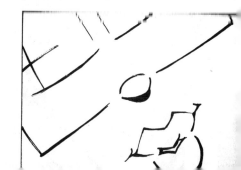

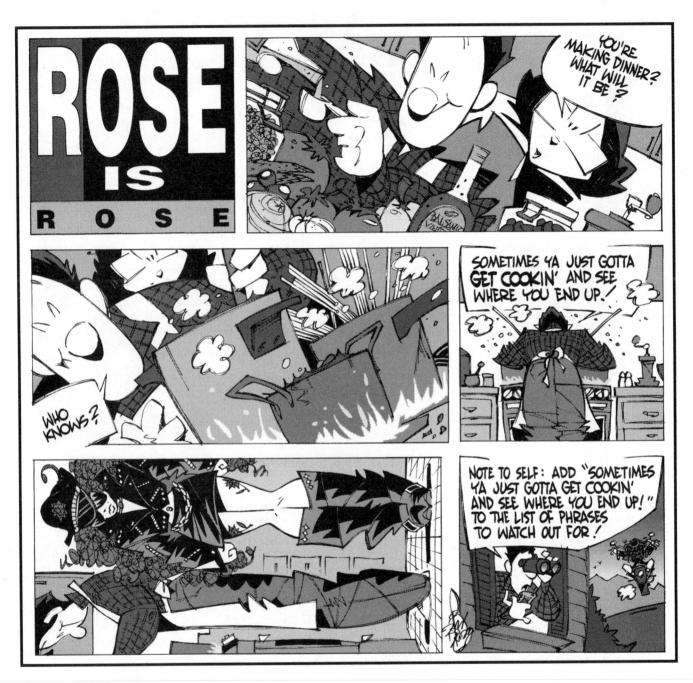

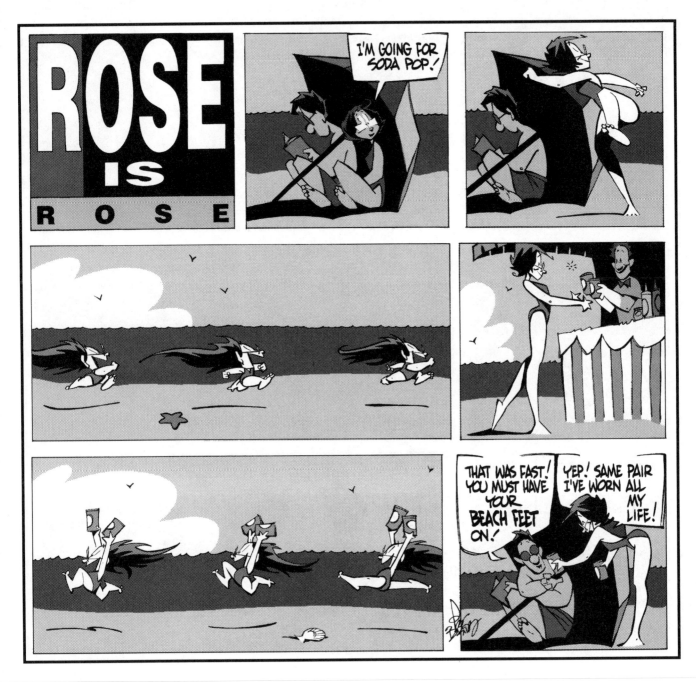

Flip the page corners
and watch both sides!

**Flip the page corners
and watch both sides!**

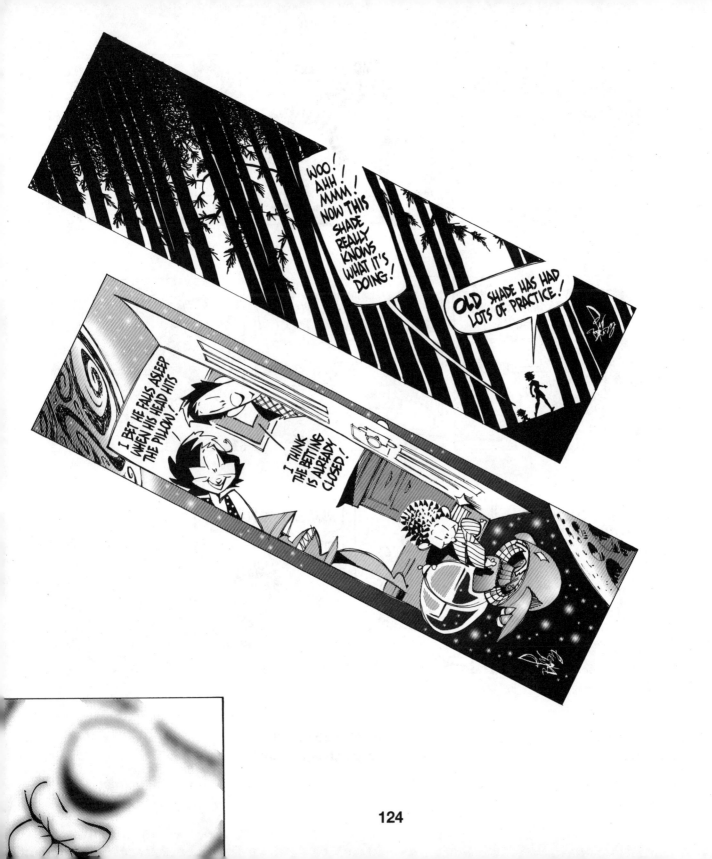

126